HAL LEONARD
**STUDENT
PIANO
LIBRARY**

Popular Piano Solos
For All Piano Methods

Table of Contents

ISBN 978-0-7935-7725-5

Visit Hal Leonard Online at
www.halleonard.com

Contact us:
Hal Leonard
7777 West Bluemound Road
Milwaukee, WI 53213
Email: info@halleonard.com

In Europe, contact:
Hal Leonard Europe Limited
42 Wigmore Street
Marylebone, London, W1U 2RN
Email: info@halleonardeurope.com

In Australia, contact:
Hal Leonard Australia Pty. Ltd.
4 Lentara Court
Cheltenham, Victoria, 3192 Australia
Email: info@halleonard.com.au

Can You Feel the Love Tonight

from Walt Disney Pictures' THE LION KING

Music by Elton John
Lyrics by Tim Rice
Arranged by Phillip Keveren

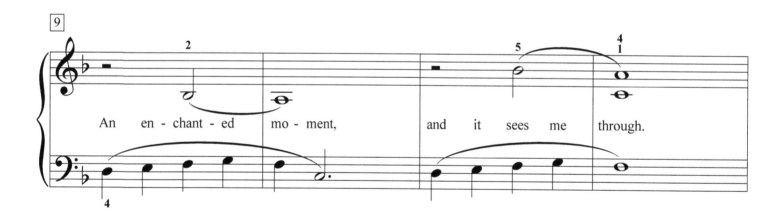

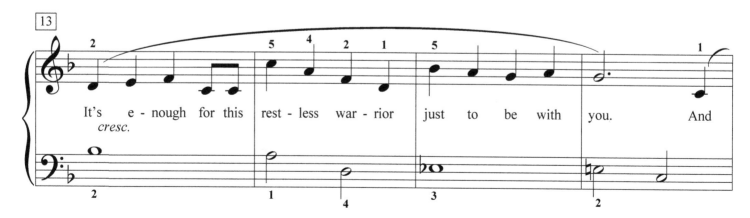

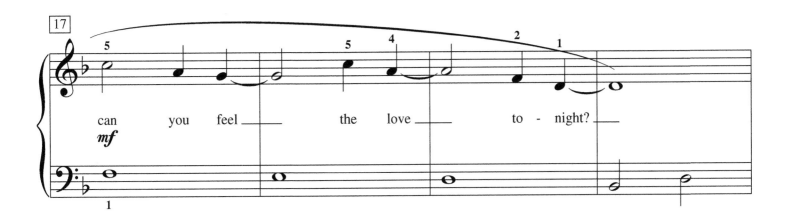

can you feel ____ the love ____ to - night? ____

mf

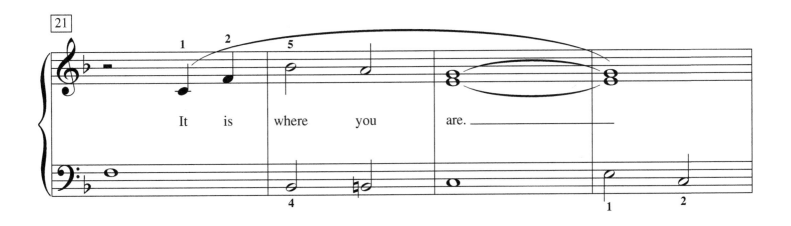

It is where you are. ____

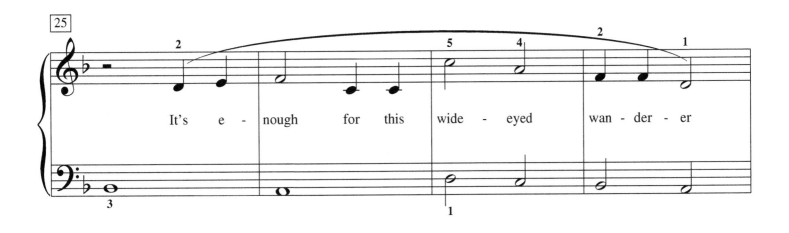

It's e - nough for this wide - eyed wan - der - er

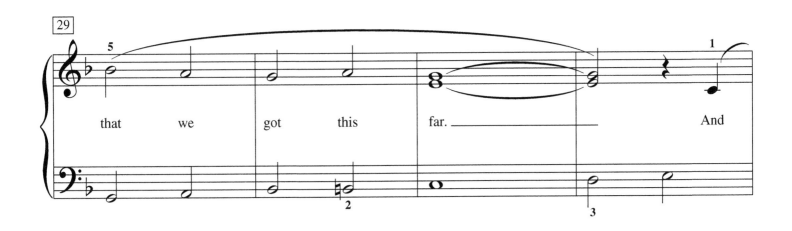

that we got this far. ____ And

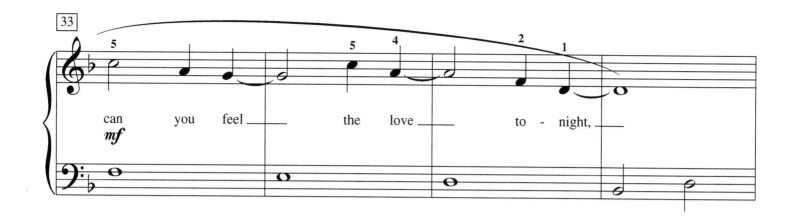

can you feel ___ the love ___ to - night, ___

mf

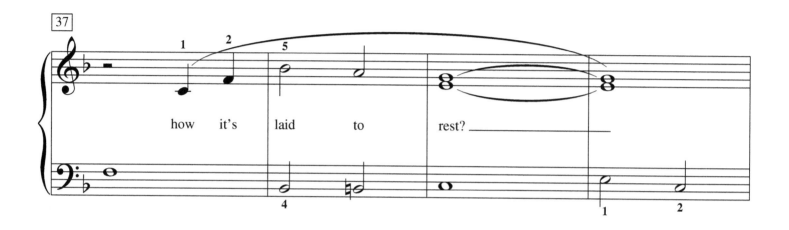

how it's laid to rest? ___

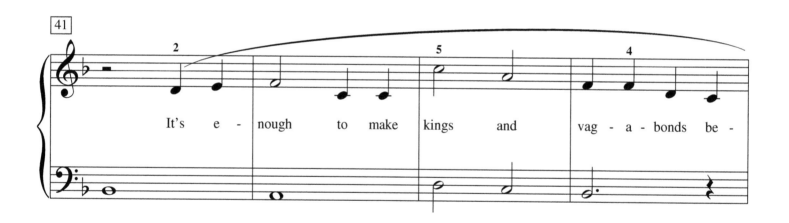

It's e - nough to make kings and vag - a - bonds be -

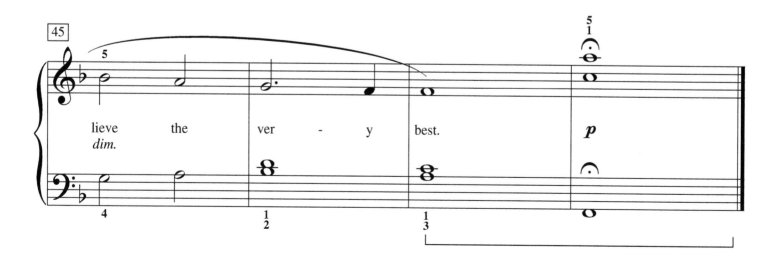

lieve the ver - y best.

dim.

p

Bubbly

Words and Music by Colbie Caillat
and Jason Reeves
Arranged by Mona Rejino

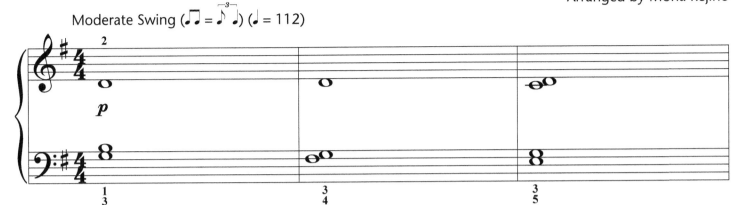

toes and I crin-kle my nose. Wher-ev - er it goes, __ I al - ways

mf

know that you make me smile. Please stay for a while now. Just take your

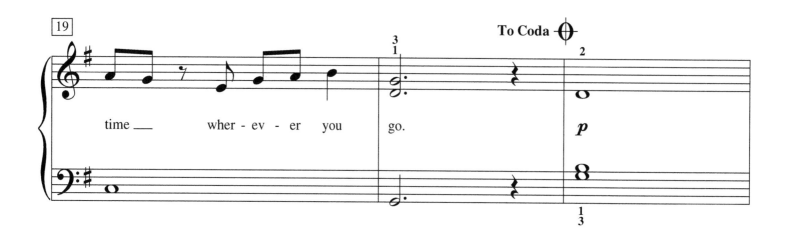

To Coda

time __ wher-ev - er you go.

p

The rain is fall - in' on my win-dow pane, but we are hid - in' in a

saf - er place. Un - der cov - er, stay - in' dry and warm,

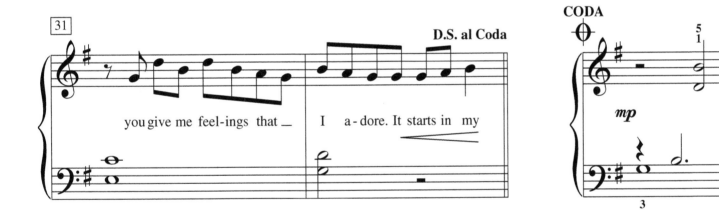

you give me feel-ings that __ I a - dore. It starts in my

D.S. al Coda

CODA

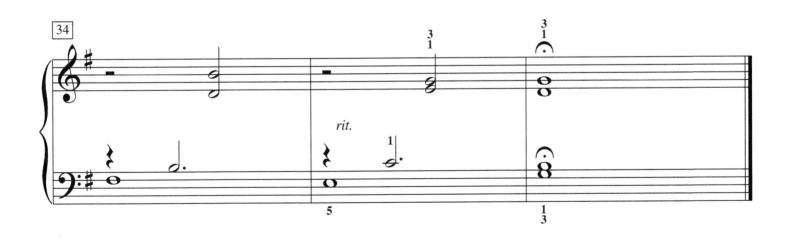

rit.

Castle on a Cloud

from LES MISÉRABLES

Music by Claude-Michel Schönberg
Lyrics by Alain Boublil,
Jean-Marc Natel and Herbert Kretzmer
Arranged by Mona Rejino

Smoothly, with expression (♩ = 84)

There is a cas - tle on a cloud.
There is a room that's full of toys.

I like to go there in my sleep.
There are a hun - dred boys and girls.

Aren't an - y floors for me to
No - bod - y shouts or talks too

I know a place where no one's lost. I know a place where no one

mp a tempo

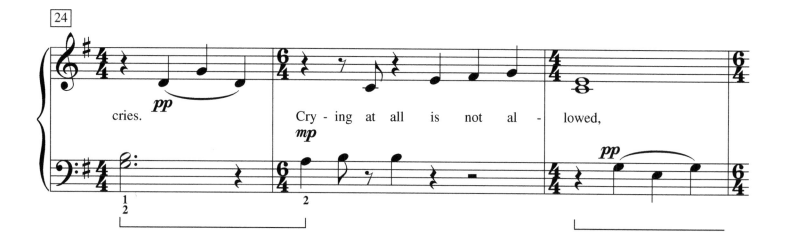

cries. *pp* Cry - ing at all is not al - lowed,

mp

pp

not in my cas - tle on a cloud. *p*

mp

Both hands 8va

(Both hands 8va)

rit.

L.H.

pp

Heart and Soul

from the Paramount Short Subject A SONG IS BORN

Words by Frank Loesser
Music by Hoagy Carmichael
Arranged by Phillip Keveren

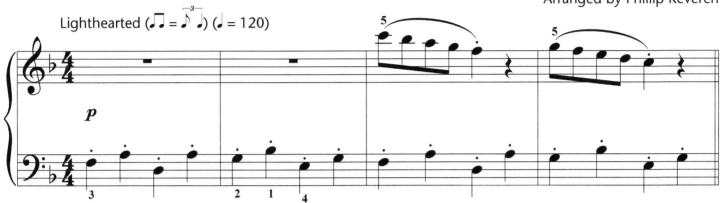

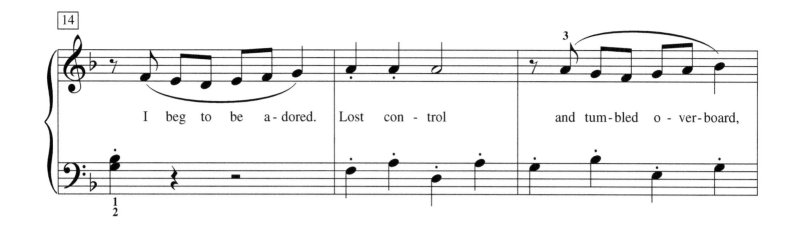

I beg to be a - dored. Lost con - trol and tum - bled o - ver-board,

glad - ly, that mag - ic night we kissed there in the

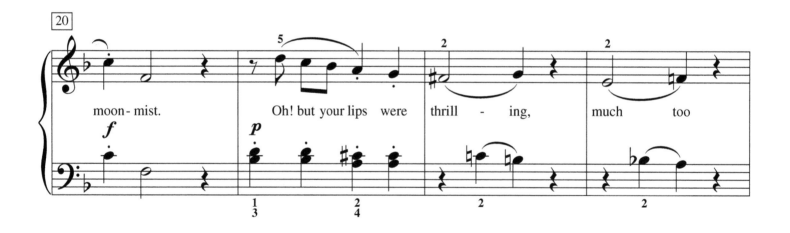

moon - mist. Oh! but your lips were thrill - ing, much too

thrill - ing. Nev - er be - fore were mine so strange - ly

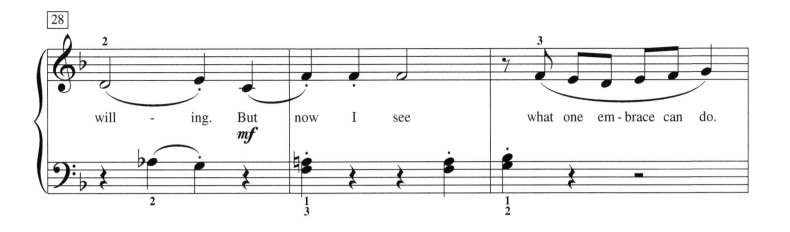

will - ing. But now I see   what one em-brace can do.

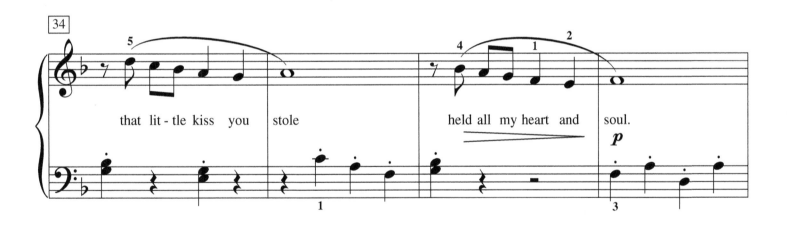

Look at me,   it's got me lov-ing you mad - ly,

that lit - tle kiss you stole   held all my heart and soul.

Firework

Words and Music by Katy Perry,
Mikkel Eriksen, Tor Erik Hermansen,
Esther Dean and Sandy Wilhelm
Arranged by Mona Rejino

Moderately fast (♩ = 120)

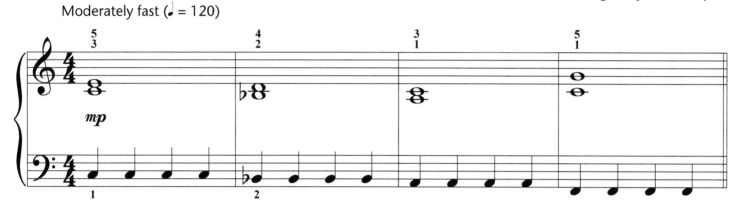

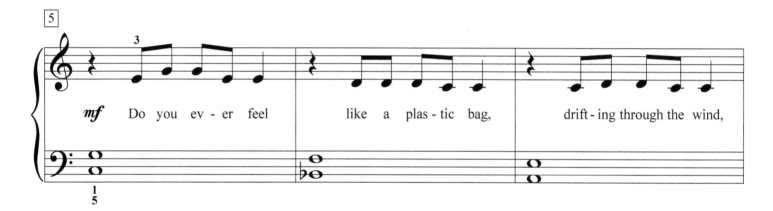

14

al - read - y bur - ied deep, six feet un - der screams, but no one seems to hear a thing?

Do you know that there's still a chance for you? 'Cause there's a spark in you.

You just got - ta ig - nite ___ the light ___ and let ___

___ it shine. ___ Just own ___ the night ___

like the Fourth _____ of Ju - ly. _____ 'Cause, ba - by, you're a

fire - work. _____ Come on, show 'em what you're worth. _

_____ Make 'em go, _____ "Ah, ah, _____ ah," as you shoot a - cross the

sky - y - y. Ba - by, you're a fire - work. _

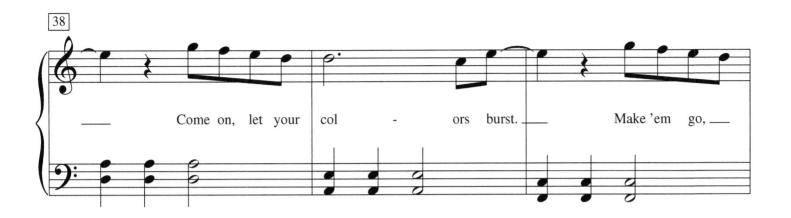

Come on, let your col - ors burst. ___ Make 'em go, ___

"Ah, ah, ___ ah." You're gon - na leave 'em all in awe, awe, ___ awe.

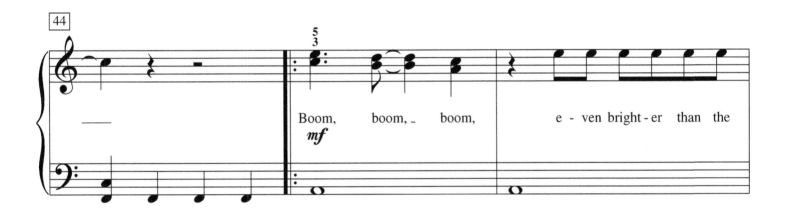

___ Boom, boom, ___ boom, e - ven bright - er than the

mf

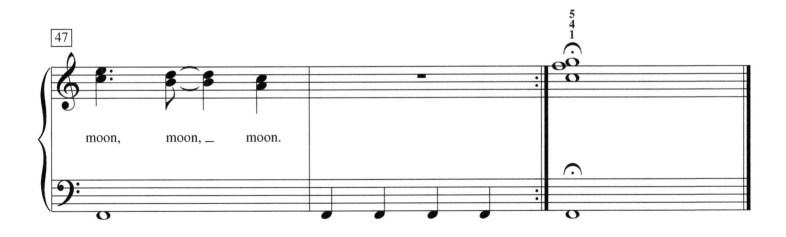

moon, moon, ___ moon.

Hallelujah

Words and Music by
Leonard Cohen
Arranged by Fred Kern

Smoothly, in "one" (♩. = 50)

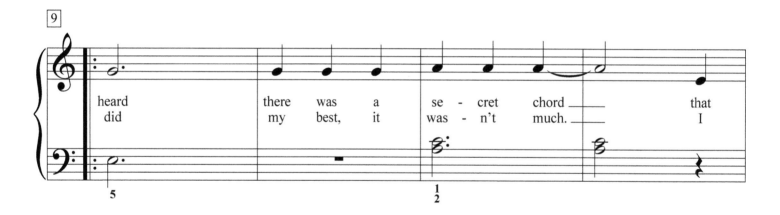

Now, I've
heard there was a se - cret chord ___ that
did my best, it was - n't much. ___ I

Accompaniment (Student plays one octave higher than written.)

Smoothly, in "one" (♩. = 50)

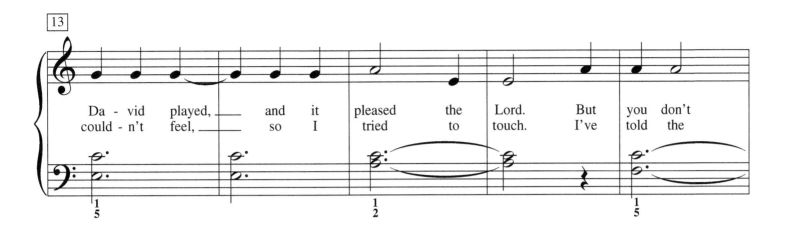

David played, ___ and it pleased the Lord. But you don't
could - n't feel, ___ so I tried the to touch. I've told the

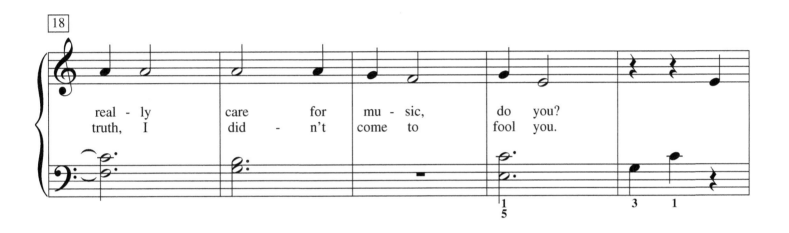

real - ly care for mu - sic, do you?
truth, I did - n't come to fool you.

It goes like this: the
And e - ven though it

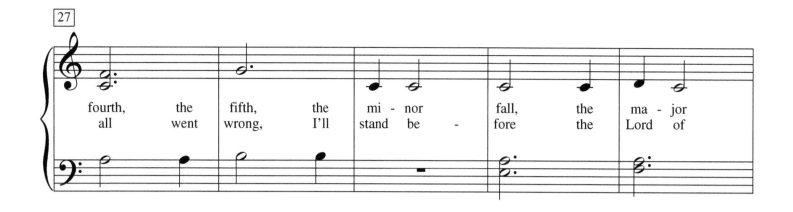

fourth, the fifth, the mi - nor fall, the ma - jor
all went wrong, I'll stand be - fore the Lord of

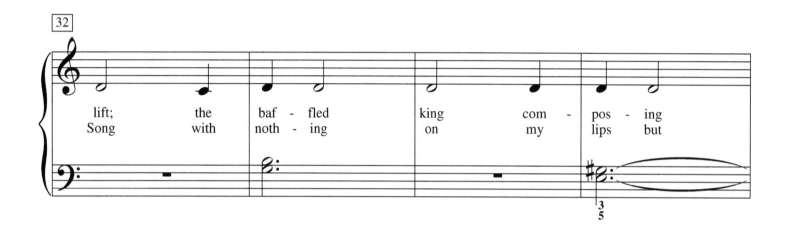

lift; the baf - fled king com - pos - ing
Song with noth - ing on my lips but

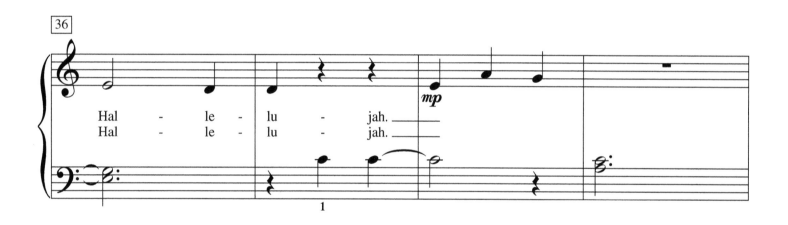

Hal - le - lu - jah.
Hal - le - lu - jah.

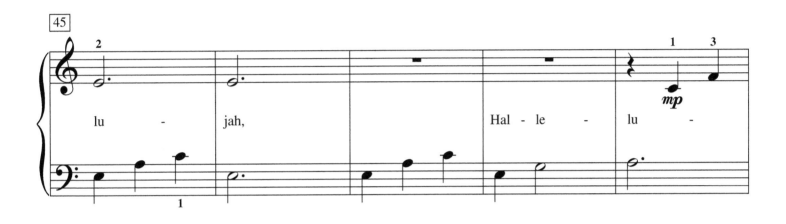

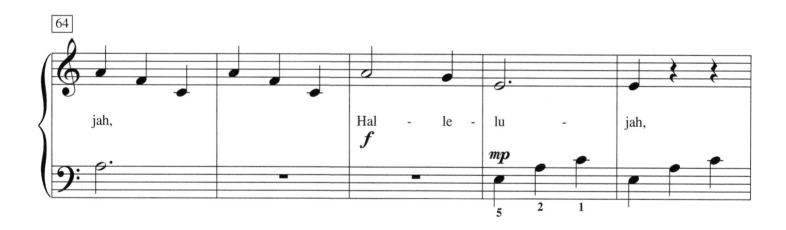

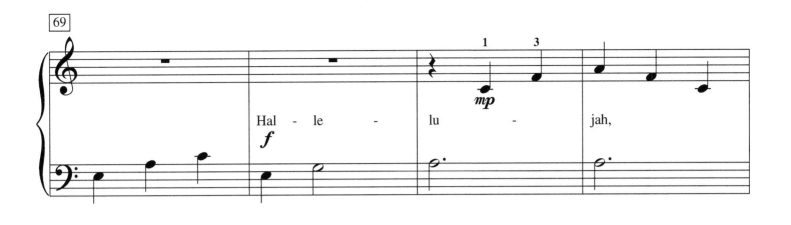

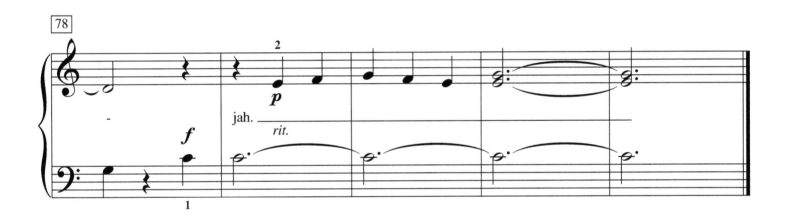

Memory
from CATS

Music by Andrew Lloyd Webber
Text by Trevor Nunn after T.S. Eliot
Arranged by Fred Kern

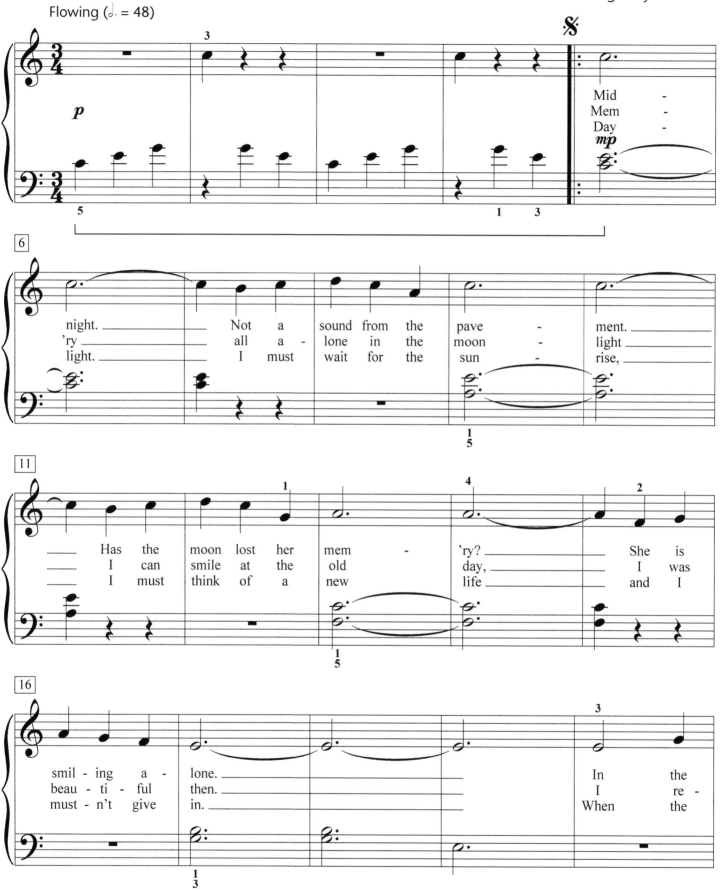

lamp - light the with - ered leaves col - lect at my
mem - ber the the time I knew what a hap - pi - ness
dawn comes, to - night I will be a mem - o - ry

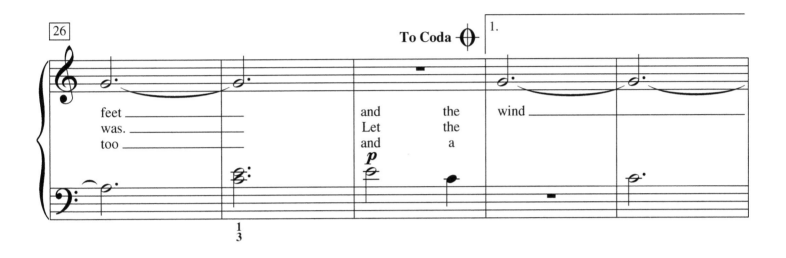

To Coda ⊕ 1.

feet _____ and the wind _____
was. _____ Let the the
too _____ and a

p

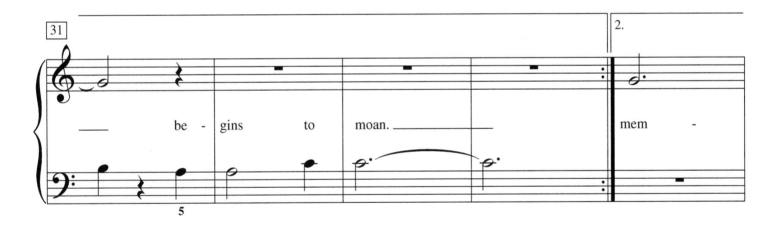

2.

_____ be - gins to moan. _____ mem -

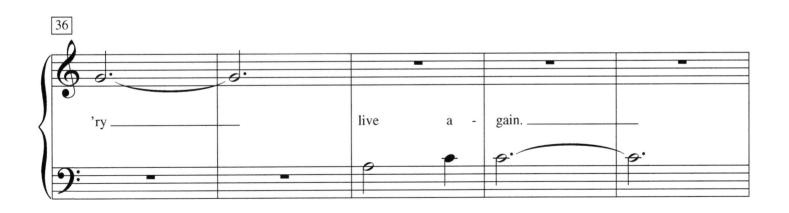

'ry _____ live a - gain. _____

25

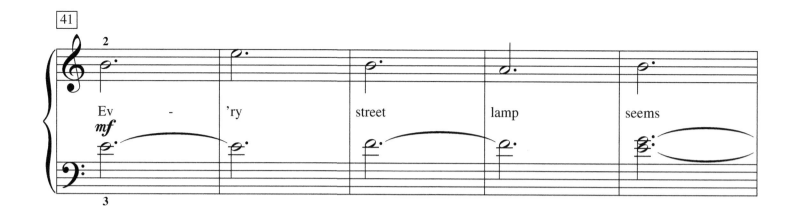

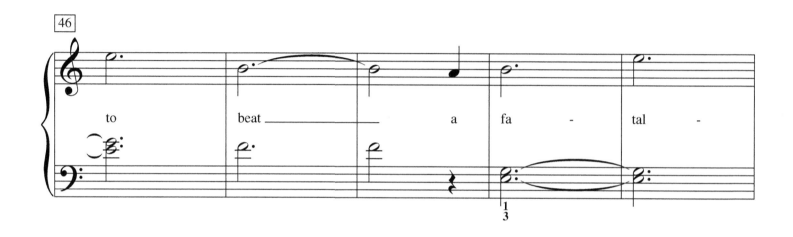

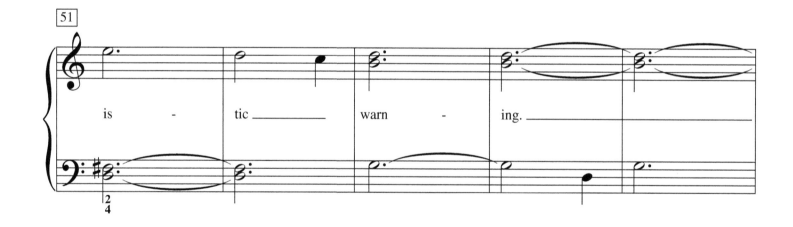

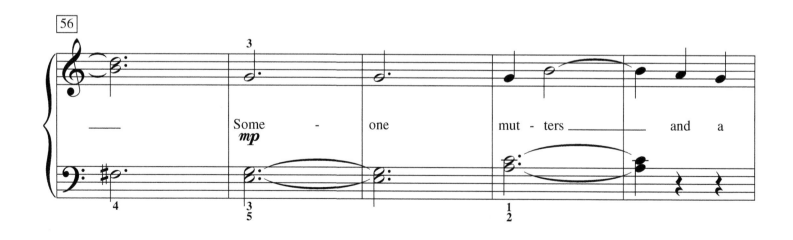

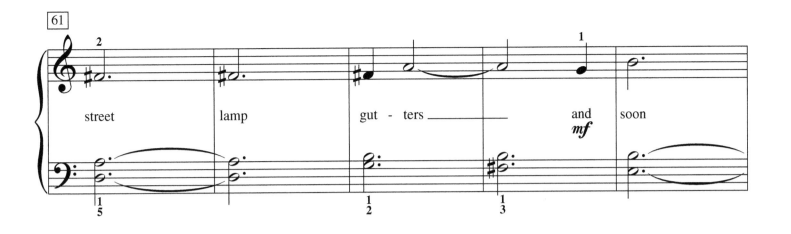

street   lamp   gut - ters _____ and soon

mf

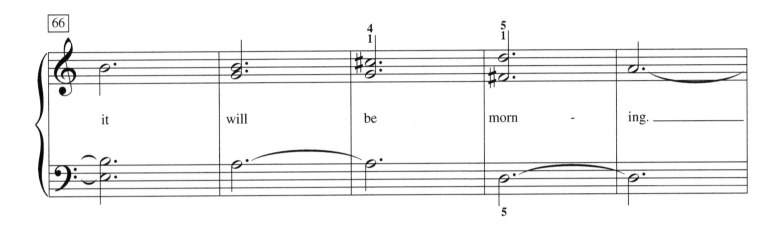

it   will   be   morn -   ing. _____

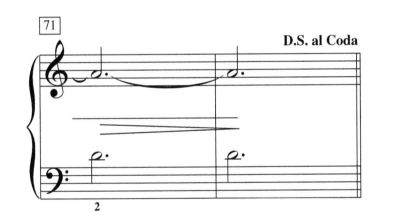

D.S. al Coda

CODA

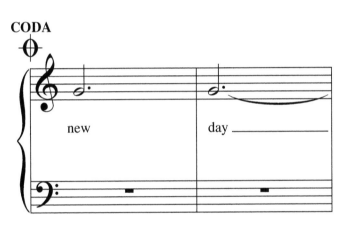

new   day _____

_____ will be - gin. _____

rit.   *pp*

Rockin' Robin

Words and Music by
J. Thomas
Arranged by Phillip Keveren

Bright Rock (♩ = 138)

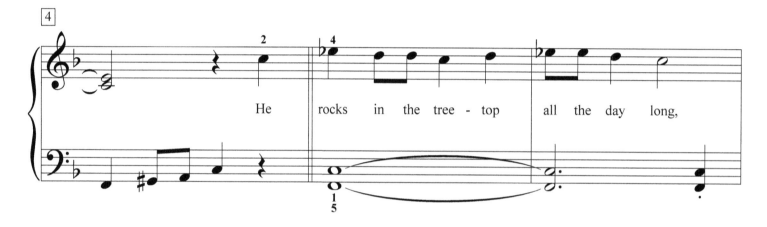

Rob - in, _____ _____ Rock - in' Rob - in. _____

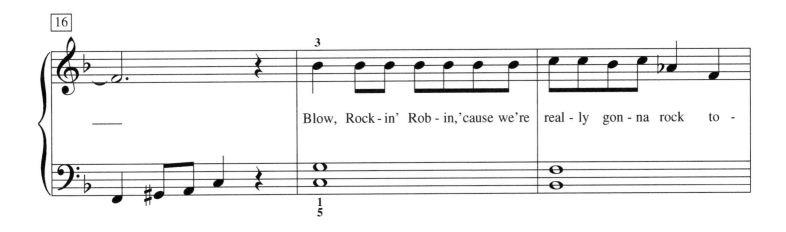

_____ Blow, Rock - in' Rob - in, 'cause we're real - ly gon - na rock to -

night. _____ _____ Ev - 'ry lit - tle swal - low,

ev - 'ry chick - a - dee, ev - 'ry lit - tle bird in the tall oak tree. The

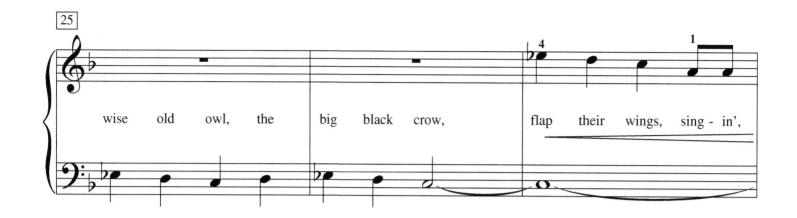

wise old owl, the big black crow, flap their wings, sing - in',

"Go, bird, go." Rock - in' Rob - in, Rock - in'

Rob - in. Blow, Rock - in' Rob - in, 'cause we're

real - ly gon - na rock to - night.

Skyfall

from the Motion Picture SKYFALL

Words and Music by Adele Adkins
and Paul Epworth
Arranged by Mona Rejino

Moderately slow, mysterious (♩ = 72)

This is the end.

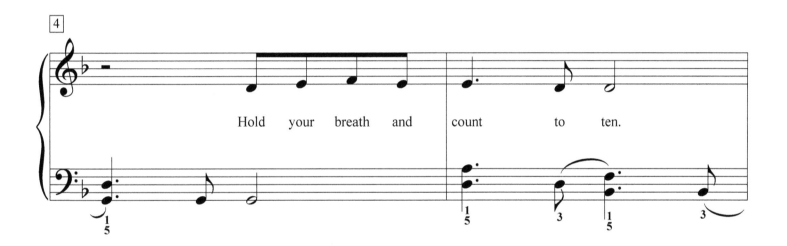

Hold your breath and count to ten.

Feel the earth move and then _____ hear my heart

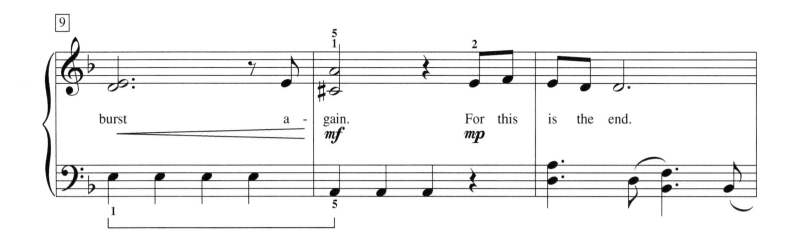

burst a - gain. For this is the end.

I've drowned and dreamt this mo - ment.

So o - ver-due I owe them. Swept a - way, I'm

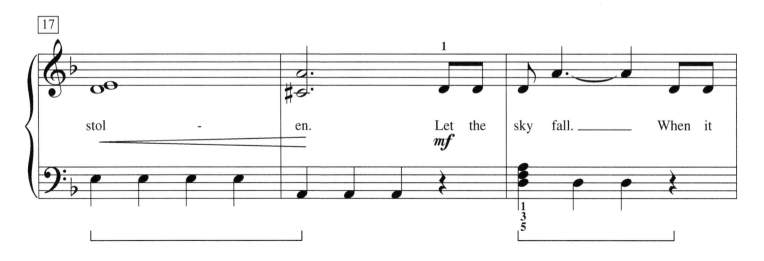

stol - en. Let the sky fall. When it

True Colors

Words and Music by Billy Steinberg
and Tom Kelly
Arranged by Fred Kern

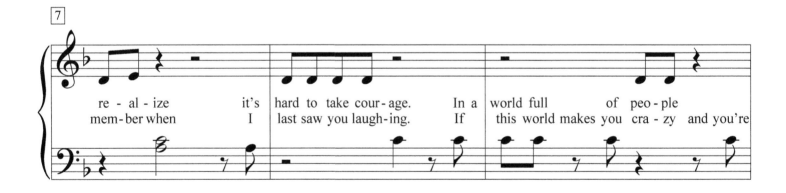

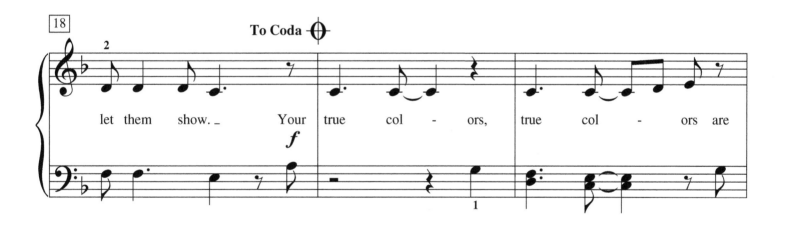

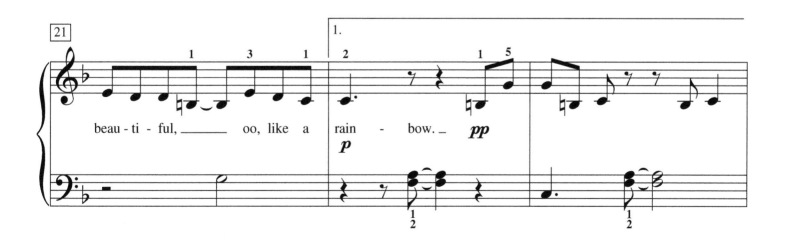

Show me your rain - bow. _ **pp**
mf **p**

D.S. al Coda
(2nd verse)

p

Show me your
mp

CODA

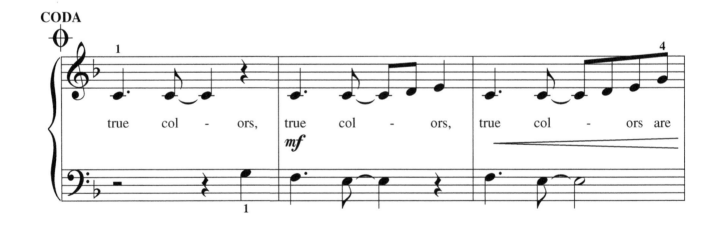

true col - ors, true col - ors, true col - ors are
mf

shin - ing through. _ I see your true col - ors and that's why I love _ you. So,
f

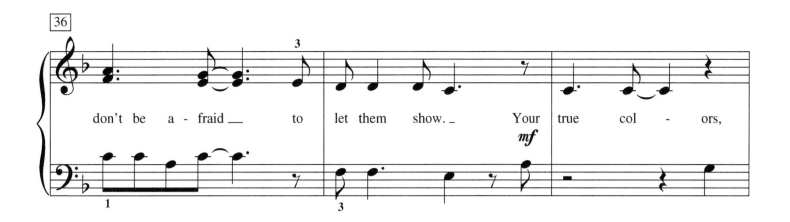

don't be a - fraid __ to let them show. _ Your true col - ors,

true col - ors are beau - ti - ful _____ like a rain - bow. _

Hal Leonard Student Piano Library

The Hal Leonard Student Piano Library has great music and solid pedagogy delivered in a truly creative and comprehensive method. It's that simple. A creative approach to learning using solid pedagogy and the best music produces skilled musicians! Great music means motivated students, inspired teachers and delighted parents. It's a method that encourages practice, progress, confidence, and best of all – success.

PIANO LESSONS BOOK 1
00296177 Book/Online Audio $9.99
00296001 Book Only $7.99

PIANO PRACTICE GAMES BOOK 1
00296002 .... $7.99

PIANO SOLOS BOOK 1
00296568 Book/Online Audio $9.99
00296003 Book Only $7.99

PIANO THEORY WORKBOOK BOOK 1
00296023 .... $7.50

PIANO TECHNIQUE BOOK 1
00296563 Book/Online Audio $8.99
00296105 Book Only $7.99

NOTESPELLER FOR PIANO BOOK 1
00296088 .... $7.99

TEACHER'S GUIDE BOOK 1
00296048 .... $7.99

PIANO LESSONS BOOK 2
00296178 Book/Online Audio $9.99
00296006 Book Only $7.99

PIANO PRACTICE GAMES BOOK 2
00296007 .... $8.99

PIANO SOLOS BOOK 2
00296569 Book/Online Audio $8.99
00296008 Book Only $7.99

PIANO THEORY WORKBOOK BOOK 2
00296024 .... $7.99

PIANO TECHNIQUE BOOK 2
00296564 Book/Online Audio $8.99
00296106 Book Only $7.99

NOTESPELLER FOR PIANO BOOK 2
00296089 .... $6.99

PIANO LESSONS BOOK 3
00296179 Book/Online Audio $9.99
00296011 Book Only $7.99

PIANO PRACTICE GAMES BOOK 3
00296012 .... $7.99

PIANO SOLOS BOOK 3
00296570 Book/Online Audio $8.99
00296013 Book Only $7.99

PIANO THEORY WORKBOOK BOOK 3
00296025 .... $7.99

PIANO TECHNIQUE BOOK 3
00296565 Book/Enhanced CD Pack $8.99
00296114 Book Only $7.99

NOTESPELLER FOR PIANO BOOK 3
00296167 .... $7.99

PIANO LESSONS BOOK 4
00296180 Book/Online Audio $9.99
00296026 Book Only $7.99

PIANO PRACTICE GAMES BOOK 4
00296027 .... $6.99

PIANO SOLOS BOOK 4
00296571 Book/Online Audio $8.99
00296028 Book Only $7.99

PIANO THEORY WORKBOOK BOOK 4
00296038 .... $7.99

PIANO TECHNIQUE BOOK 4
00296566 Book/Online Audio $8.99
00296115 Book Only $7.99

PIANO LESSONS BOOK 5
00296181 Book/Online Audio $9.99
00296041 Book Only $8.99

PIANO SOLOS BOOK 5
00296572 Book/Online Audio $9.99
00296043 Book Only $7.99

PIANO THEORY WORKBOOK BOOK 5
00296042 .... $8.99

PIANO TECHNIQUE BOOK 5
00296567 Book/Online Audio $8.99
00296116 Book Only $8.99

ALL-IN-ONE PIANO LESSONS
00296761 Book A – Book/Online Audio $10.99
00296776 Book B – Book/Online Audio $10.99
00296851 Book C – Book/Online Audio $10.99
00296852 Book D – Book/Online Audio $10.99

Prices, contents, and availability subject to change without notice.

www.halleonard.com